The Adventures of Bella Bell
Copyright © 2023

Author, Susana Aguilar
Illustrator, Antonella Cammarano

All rights reserved. No part of this book may be reproduced or used in any manner without the written permission of the copyright owner, except for the use of brief quotations in a book review.

The Adventures of Bella Bell

Written by Susana Aguilar
Illustrated by Antonella Cammarano

Dedicated to all the firsts this world has to offer.

Bella Bell Goes to the Zoo

  Bella Bell Goes to the Moon

  Bella Bell Goes to the Beach

  Bella Bell and the Magnifying Glass

  Kingdom Animalia

  Glossary
Words in bold can be found in the glossary.

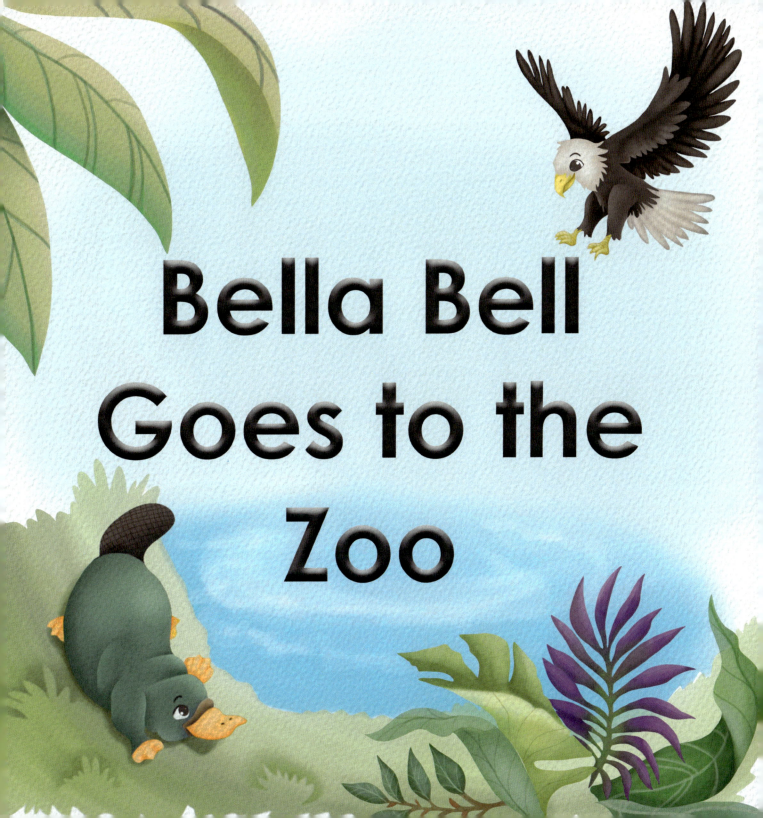

The yellow sun is shining through.
What will I wear?
I think I will dress in blue for my day at the zoo.
Just imagine all of the **astonishing** things we will see and the **impressive** friends we will meet.

Hello, what are the fees for 3 tickets please?

This one is on the house.
Come through, come inside.
Follow me, I'm your **guide**.
Ever seen a bird's eye view?
Welcome to the **Zany** Zoo!

Hi, I'm Bella Bell.
This is Morrison, and this is Maná.
They are pugs and give **magical** hugs.
We are the best of friends. That is what makes us **special**.
I love dogs and all animals too. I'm here to learn what's **unique** about you.

I'm Elario, the **enthralling** eagle.
I've got tough talons and a big beak.
You can find me here every day of the week.
Put my eyes to the test. My **vision** is the best.
Watch me swoop down on **prey** on any given day.
Soaring through the air at lightning **speed**.
Indeed, a **breed** of flight and great height, I claim to be.
Let me show you around, let me show you the way.
Meet my friends; all so **fantastic** in their own **special** ways.

Did you Know: Eagles can grow up to four feet tall. This is about as tall as an 8-year-old child. Eagle eyes have two centers of focus. This allows them to see forward and sideways at the same time. The vision of an eagle is much more **powerful** than that of a human.

Eagles can see about eight times as far as a human can. Eagles have excellent eyesight and can spot small **prey** from great heights. They dive at an **incredible speed** and use their talons to snatch the prey from the ground. Bald Eagles can dive down at a speed of 100 miles per hour. In comparison, the fastest human can run at about 28 miles per hour.

Golden Eagles can dive at speeds of up to 200 miles per hour. Eagles have strong muscular legs, powerful talons (claws), and large hooked beaks. Eagles can carry about 5 pounds of weight with their talons. Their beaks and talons are made out of Keratin; just like human hair and human nails are made out of keratin.

This means that their beaks and talons never grow old and continue to grow throughout their lifetime. Their talons are curved and sharp for catching and holding down their prey, while their beak enables them to rip the flesh from their prey.

Eagles are birds of prey, which means they hunt for prey that is relatively large in comparison to the hunter. Golden eagles are the largest bird of prey.

Did you know: There are two **species** of gorillas in the world: the eastern gorilla and the western gorilla. There are four subspecies of gorillas on the planet: mountain gorilla, eastern lowland gorilla, western lowland gorilla, and cross river gorilla.

A group of gorillas is called a "troop." A troop typically consists of a **dominant** male known as a silverback, a few females, and their **offspring**. A silverback gorilla can grow to be about 6 feet tall and weigh around 500 pounds. A troop can have as little as five members or as many as fifty members. Gorillas and humans are very closely related. We share at least 95% of our DNA (deoxyribonucleic acid is the molecule that contains the genetic code of organisms).

Gorillas have opposable thumbs (able to move and touch the other fingers on the same hand) just like we do. Their sight, hearing, and smell are closely similar to our **senses**. Just like human babies, gorillas are helpless at birth and need to be nurtured (to care for and encourage growth and development) by their mother for the first couple years of their lives. Gorillas perceive the world very much like humans do. They live in largely permanent family groups.

Their life expectancy is about the same as ours. Gorillas are both quadrupedal and bipedal walkers. Quadrupeds use both their hands and feet to walk. Bipeds only use two legs to walk. Gorillas are known to make tools and weapons. They use sticks to make hammers and spears. They use logs as ladders. These makeshift tools aid the Gorilla's survival in **scavenging** for food. Gorillas are **herbivores** for the most part. They feed on plants, fruits, and the occasional insect.

It is a pleasure to meet you. I'm Eve, the **extraordinary** elephant.
I am the largest animal to **roam** land, to see me in the **wild** is really quite grand.
I have a long nose, although I suppose it acts more like a hand
when it grabs on command.
I call it a trunk, and it helps me eat a **colossal** chunk.
About 300 pounds of food in one day. What can I say?
I'm an **exuberant** beast who sure loves to **feast**.

Did you know: There are two **species** of elephants: African and Asian. Elephants can grow up to 13 feet tall, 21 feet long, and weigh up to 14,000 pounds. In comparison, the average family car weighs about 4,000 pounds. They have a long, muscular nose called a trunk, which can grow up to 7 feet long.

Their trunk alone can grow to be longer than the height of the average man. Elephants have about 40,000 muscles in their trunks. An elephant has more muscles in its trunk than in the rest of its body. Elephants use their trunks to grab things, drink water, and as a snorkel. Female elephants have the longest pregnancy of all mammals. They carry their young for twenty-two months before giving birth.

In comparison, a human woman is pregnant for about nine months. Baby elephants are called calves. Calves can stand within minutes and walk within hours of their birth.

Whereas, human babies take their first steps at 12 months on average. Elephants have the longest eyelashes in the world. Their eyelashes can grow up to five inches. Elephants have very thick and wrinkly skin, as thick as an inch. The thickness and wrinkles help elephants **retain** moisture and water.

Elephants have **extraordinary** memories. They have the largest brain size and temporal lobe among land mammals. The temporal lobe is the part of the cerebral cortex devoted to communication, language, spatial memory, and **cognition**.

Good day, I am Adri, the **amazing** alligator.
I am very toothy and very long, scaly, and live in a swamp.
I have about 80 teeth because I love to eat.
But do not mistake me and take me for a **clever** crocodile.
The smile of a crocodile is toothier and long.
Its closed mouth will reveal a great deal. Its underneath and top teeth!
My smile will only show the top row.
Still in doubt? Just look at the **snout**.

Did you know: Alligators and crocodiles are from the same scientific order but from different families. Alligators and crocodiles are reptiles. Reptiles are 4 legged **vertebrate** animals. The majority of reptiles lay eggs and breathe through **lungs**. They are cold-blooded and have scaly skin. You can typically tell alligators and crocodiles apart by looking at their **snout**.

Alligators have a wide rounded U-shaped snout, while crocodiles have a pointy triangular V-shaped snout. Alligators replace their teeth as they fall out. An alligator can go through 3,000 teeth in their lifetime, whereas crocodiles can go through 8,000 teeth in their lifetime. Alligators can stay underwater for up to twenty-four hours by holding their breath.

Alligators can grow to be about 15 feet long. Saltwater Crocodiles are the largest reptiles in the world. They can grow up to 22 feet in **length**. The Saltwater Crocodile has the strongest bite of any animal on the planet. Its bite has a force of about 4,000 pounds per square inch. PSI or pound per square inch is the pressure resulting from a force of one pound-force applied to an area of one square inch. In comparison, a heavyweight boxer can punch about 1,500 pounds per square inch on average.

Hello dear!

Howdy, I'm Mork, the **magnificent** moose.
I have antlers on top of my head.
Every winter they shed, and every spring they grow back.
When I am in danger, I use them to attack.
I go for a swim on a hungry **whim**, munch on lunch at the bottom of a lake.
If the option arose for dessert or snow, below zero is where I'd go.
Freezing **temperature** is where I **thrive**, **insulated** fur is how I survive.

"Life is good in this neck of the woods."

Did you know: Moose are the largest **species** of deer in the world. They can grow to be about 7 feet tall, 10 feet long, and weigh up to 1,500 pounds. Moose are **herbivores** and eat about 70 pounds of plants in one day. In comparison, the average person eats about 4 pounds of food a day. Only male moose have antlers. When their antlers shed, other animals like squirrels, foxes, and bears eat the antlers.

The antlers are made out of calcium, phosphorus, and mineral salt nutrients. The size of the antlers can give away their age. Every year, young moose antlers grow in size.

Full-grown antlers can weigh up to 40 pounds. The size of their antlers can determine **dominance**. Moose with smaller antlers will typically back off if challenged. As a moose enters old age, its antlers become misshapen. Moose are strong swimmers. They can swim for several miles at a time and reach **speeds** of 6 miles per hour. They can dive as deep as 20 feet and eat underwater if they find **vegetation**. Moose have cloven hooves (the horny part of the foot), which means their hooves are split. Their hooves help them walk in the snow as deep as 3 feet for several months.

The split in their hooves allow them to stay on top of the snow and not sink in. Their sharp hooves are great for fighting off **predators**. Moose love cold weather and will feel most comfortable at **temperatures** below 23 degrees **Fahrenheit**.

They have **insulated** fur and **hollow** hair, which helps them **retain** heat. Their **snout** also helps keep them warm. When humans inhale cold air, it goes directly into our **lungs**. However, the **nasal** passage of a moose forces air through a long, winding path that heats the air before it reaches their lungs.

I am Bella Bell, and who are you?

I am Karim, the **knockout** kangaroo.
Take a seat. Isn't it neat that I can leap up to 30 feet in a single bound?
How does that sound? Get a load of this.
When something's amiss, it's not my front legs but my **hind** that get me out of a **bind**.
I use a slick trick. My feet pound the ground, and I give a quick karate kick.

Did you know: Kangaroos have a **powerful** kick. A kangaroo kick has a force of 850 pounds per square inch. Their **hind** legs are powerful, whereas their front legs are much smaller. If **threatened**, kangaroos will stomp the ground and kick with their strong feet as a warning.

Kangaroos have long and strong tails. They use their tails to balance while leaping. Female kangaroos have a pouch in their belly. However, they aren't born with the pouch. The pouch develops as they grow. This pouch or fold in the skin is used to carry their young for the first few months of their lives. Newborn kangaroos are called joeys. Joeys are about an inch long, hairless, and blind at birth. Joeys can find and crawl into their mother's pouch on their own immediately after birth. Joeys live in their mother's pouch for about 10 months. The pouch is their home, and so here is where the joey will poop and urinate for the first few months of its life.

The pouch opens upwards and has to be cleaned regularly. The mother kangaroo will clean her pouch by sticking her **snout** in and licking out all the dirt. Kangaroos are the tallest of all marsupials (a mammal, born incompletely developed, and are typically carried and **suckled** in a pouch on the mother's belly), standing at up to 8 feet tall.

Marsupials are characterized as pouched mammals, having short **gestation** periods, with young born in an embryonic state; and a **lengthy lactation** period, during which the young remain in the pouch.

SSSalutations, I'm SSStef the ssslithering sssnake.
I cause no harm. My kind is mostly charm.
No legs and no arms, but do not be alarmed.
Ssstrong muscles help me hustle.
I move and I groove.
sssquirm, ssslide, sssscuttle, ssslink and ssslither
My skin will wither, but do not be ssstartled.
As my body **expands**, you will soon understand, it's all part of a master plan.

Did you know: There are more than 3,000 **species** of snakes in the world. About 600 of these species are **venomous**. Snakes are not able to blink, because they don't have eyelids. Snakes do not chew their **prey**; they swallow it whole. They have flexible (bending easily without breaking) jaws that help them eat prey bigger than their head. Some species wrap their body around their prey to squeeze and **suffocate** them. Snakes smell with their Jacobson's organ.

This organ is found on the roof of their mouth. Snakes stick their tongues out to pick up scents in the air then dart their tongue into their Jacobson organ. Snakes use their muscles and scales to push off bumps and **surfaces** that allow them to move and **slither**.

They continuously outgrow their skin. Every year, the old skin sheds, so that new skin can grow to fit their bodies. Shedding also helps get rid of harmful **parasites**. Snakes can lift about 33% of their bodies off the ground while slithering. They lunge their bodies forward and appear to be jumping. The reticulated python is the longest snake, reaching **lengths** of about 33 feet.

In comparison, the average bus is about 40 feet long. The anaconda is the heaviest snake, weighing about 500 pounds. The black mamba is the fastest snake in the world reaching **speeds** of about 12 miles per hour. The black mamba and the inland taipan are two of the world's deadliest snakes.

What a **marvelous** day at the zoo! If one thing is true, it's that we have a **remarkable** crew. We are all different. All unalike, but one thing is certain. We each have our own **strength**, no matter our **length**, shape, or size. The world wouldn't **function** without you or them. Consider yourself a **precious gem**!

Did you know:

1. Giraffes are the tallest animals on the planet. They can grow to be about 18 feet tall. In comparison, the tallest man in the world is 8 feet and 2 inches tall. Giraffes are known to sleep standing up and with their eyes open.

2.There are two types of camels: dromedary camels, which have one hump, and bactrian camels, which have two humps. Camels can go several months without drinking water. Camels store fat in their humps to use when food is scarce.

3. The Ostrich is the world's largest bird at about 9 feet tall. Although ostriches cannot fly, they are very fast, reaching **speeds** of up to 45 miles per hour. Ostriches have 2 finger claws on each foot that help them deliver a **powerful** kick at a force of about 2,000 pounds per square inch.

4. Owls do not actually have eyeballs. They have tubed eyes that are held in place by bone. Owls cannot move their eyes at all. To look around, an owl must rotate its head. Owls can turn their necks about 270 degrees in either direction and 90 degrees up-and-down, without moving their shoulders. In comparison, humans can rotate their necks 180 degrees.

5. A platypus has a body and fur like an otter, a bill and webbed feet like a duck, and a tail like a beaver. Platypus do not have teeth or a stomach. The platypus is one of only three mammals that produce venom. A male platypus delivers **venom** through ankle spurs, which can best be described as a thorn on the ankle (females aren't venomous). The platypus is one of only two types of egg-laying mammals. These traits are unusual in mammals.

6. Although bats can fly, they are mammals and not birds. Almost all bat **species** hang upside down. Bats sleep hanging upside down because they can't launch or run and take off into the air like birds can. Instead, they fall into flight. Over 300 species of fruit depend on bats for pollination (the transfer of pollen from a male part of a plant to a female part of a plant, later enabling fertilization and the production of seeds). The flying fox bat is the biggest, with a wing span of up to 6 feet.

7. Polar Bears are **marine** mammals. They depend on the ocean for their food. Their skin is black, but their hair is **translucent**. Their fur appears white because it catches and reflects light. Polar bears are excellent swimmers. They can swim for days without rest.

8. Electric eels can grow up to 8 feet in **length** and weigh up to 45 pounds. They live in freshwater, but have to come up often to breathe air. Electric eels can **release** up to 650 volts of electricity, which is 5 times the power of a U.S.A wall **socket**. This voltage is enough to knock a horse off its feet. Electric eels use their shocking abilities to stun **prey** and as a defense mechanism against **predators**.

9. There are over 5000 species of frogs. The glass frog is **unique** because of its translucent skin. Its internal organs are visible. Glass frogs are **nocturnal amphibians**. Another interesting species is the hairy frog. It has earned its nickname because of the hair-like structures covering its body. The hairy frog is also known as the horror frog or wolverine frog. It intentionally breaks its toe bones when **threatened**, which then pokes through the skin to act like claws. These bones later retract, and the damaged tissue heals.

10. Tigers are the largest cat species in the world. The Siberian tiger can weigh about 650 pounds and grow up to 13 feet in length. They are the third largest carnivore (to feed on flesh) on land after bears and polar bears. Tigers typically live a **solitary** life. A tiger's night **vision** is 6 times stronger than a human's vision.

11. Lions are the second largest cat species on Earth. Lions have the loudest roar of all big cats. It can reach 114 **decibels** and can be heard from five miles away. They live in groups called prides, which can be as large as 40 members. Female lions are the primary hunters of the pride. Lions spend up to 20 hours a day sleeping.

12. Panthers refer to 3 different types of big cats, leopards, jaguars, and cougars. Panthers are great swimmers and are one of the strongest tree-climbing big cats. They are able to jump about 20 feet **vertically** from a standing position. Their jumping abilities, strong jaws, along with excellent hearing and eyesight, make them excellent hunters.

*An **apex predator** is a species that is at the top of the food chain and does not have any natural predators in its environment. The apex predators of the world on land are: alligator snapping turtle, american alligator, american crocodile, brown bear, cape **wild** dog, cougar, eagle, giant petrel, dhole, great horned owl, jaguar, king cobra, kodiak bear, komodo dragon, lion, lynx, nile crocodile, polar bear, reticulated python, snow leopard, south polar skua, tasmanian devil, tiger, wolf.

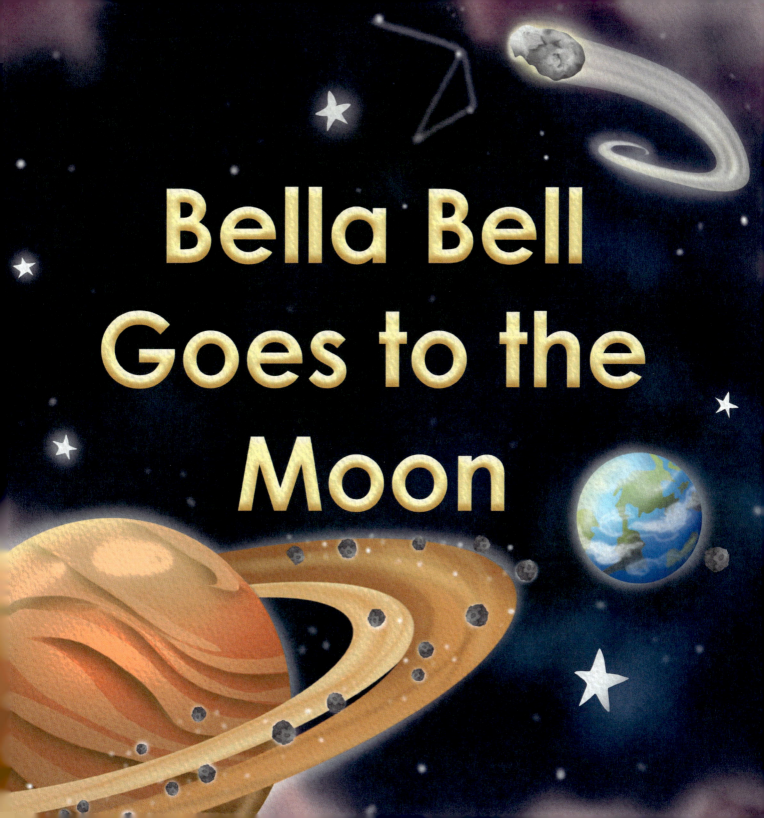

It's 8 O'clock. It's time for bed. Bella Bell must rest her head.
What will I dream about tonight?
What a bright light, such a **starry** sight, but where am I?

Greetings, I'm June, and you're on the moon.
I'm happy to meet you. Visitors are few.
Let me show you around, fun is **abound**.
Look there, that is the sun.
It is a **fiery sphere** and the reason we have heat, light, and energy every day of the year.
Jump up off the ground, see how we bounce.
What is that sound? What do I see?
I can see stars, and I can see Mars. That is Venus and that is Saturn.
Look at their **mesmerizing** pattern. I can see orange and red up ahead.

Did you know: The Solar system is made up of 8 planets that orbit (to rotate around something) the sun in a **counterclockwise** direction. The planets in the solar system are Mercury, Venus, Earth, Mars, Jupiter, Saturn, Uranus, and Neptune (in order of distance from the sun). 6 planets spin on their **axis** in a counterclockwise **motion** (west to east). The other two planets, Venus and Uranus spin on their axis in a clockwise motion (east to west). One orbit around the sun is considered one year. One rotation on its axis is considered one day. There is a small amount of gravity (force of attraction that pulls together all matter) in space compared to the amount of gravity on planet Earth. This is why you aren't being pulled down towards the ground in space like you are on Earth. There are other smaller bodies in the solar system, such as dwarf planets, asteroids (small rocky bodies orbiting the sun), meteoroids (pebble-sized asteroids or comets), stars, and comets (lumps of ice, dust, and rock that orbit the Sun). Up until the year 2006, Pluto was considered the 9th planet closest to the sun. However, in August 2006 the International Astronomical Union (IAU) changed the status of Pluto from a full-sized planet to a "dwarf planet." A full-sized planet will have the following 3 characteristics:

1. It is in orbit around the sun.
2. It has sufficient mass to assume hydrostatic equilibrium (a nearly round shape).
3. It has "cleared the neighborhood" around its orbit.

Pluto has not "cleared the neighborhood" around its orbit. Clearing the neighborhood means that the planet has become gravitationally **dominant**. There should be no other bodies of comparable size other than its own satellites or those otherwise under its gravitational influence, in its surrounding space.

1. Mercury is the closest planet to the sun. It is also the smallest planet in the solar system. Mercury's **diameter** (a straight line passing from side to side through the center of a body or figure, especially a circle or **sphere**) is about 3,031.9 miles. In comparison, the United States' distance from the west coast to the east coast is about 3,000 miles. Mercury's **surface** is covered with craters. It is a gray and rocky planet with an iron core and a thick layer of dust. Mercury does not have any moons. It takes 88 Earth days for Mercury to complete 1 orbit around the sun (A year on Mercury lasts 88 Earth days). Mercury spins counterclockwise on its axis. Mercury takes 59 Earth days to make one full rotation. A day on Mercury lasts 59 Earth days.

2. Venus is the second planet closest to the sun and the hottest of all planets. **Temperatures** can reach up to 900 degrees **Fahrenheit**. Venus is about seven times hotter than the hottest place on Earth. In comparison, Death Valley (a desert valley in Eastern California, USA) is said to be the hottest area on Earth. 134 degrees Fahrenheit is the hottest temperature ever recorded in Death Valley. Venus is a yellow planet covered with a thick **carbon dioxide** atmosphere (layer of gasses that surround a planet) and sulphuric acid clouds. Venus does not have any moons. It takes 225 Earth days for Venus to complete 1 orbit around the sun. Venus spins clockwise on its axis. A day on Venus lasts 243 Earth days. That means that a day on Venus is a little longer than a year on Venus.

3. Earth is the third planet closest to the sun. It is made up of oxygen and water. About 71% of Earth's surface is covered by water. Earth is a blue, green, brown, white, and rocky planet. It has a solid and active surface with mountains, valleys, canyons, and plains. Earth's atmosphere is made up of nitrogen and protects us from incoming meteoroids. Most meteoroids break up in our atmosphere before they can strike the surface as meteorites. Earth has 1 moon. It takes 365.25 days for Earth to complete 1 orbit around the sun. That extra 0.25 means every four years, we need to add one day to our calendar. We call it a leap day. Earth spins counterclockwise on its axis. A day on Earth lasts 24 hours.

4. Mars is the fourth planet closest to the sun. Mars is known as the Red planet. It is red because of rusty iron in the ground. It is made up of silicon, oxygen, iron, and magnesium. Mars is very dry and dusty. It is home to Volcano Olympus Mons, the highest mountain in the solar system. Mars has two moons. It takes Mars 687 Earth days to complete 1 orbit around the sun. Mars spins counterclockwise on its axis. One day on Mars lasts 24 hours and 36 minutes.

5. Jupiter is the fifth planet closest to the sun. It is the biggest planet in the solar system with a diameter of 86,881 miles. Jupiter has faint rings and swirling stripes. It is orange, white, and brown. Jupiter is a giant gas planet made up of hydrogen and helium. It has 79 moons. It takes Jupiter 12 Earth years to complete 1 orbit around the sun. It spins counterclockwise on its axis. Jupiter completes its rotation in 9 hours and 56 minutes. It is the fastest rotation of all planets, which means it has the shortest day of all planets.

6. Saturn is the sixth planet closest to the sun. Saturn is surrounded by icy, rocky, and dusty rings. Its rings are the most clearly visible of all planets. Saturn is yellow and brown. It is made up of hydrogen and helium. Saturn has 82 moons and the most moons of all planets. It takes Saturn 29.5 Earth years to complete 1 orbit around the sun. Saturn spins **counterclockwise** on its **axis**. A day on Saturn lasts 10 hours and 42 minutes.

7. Uranus is the seventh planet closest to the sun and the coldest of all planets. The coldest **temperature** ever recorded on Uranus reached -371 degrees **Fahrenheit**. In comparison, the coldest place on Earth is Antarctica with temperatures averaging about -144 degrees Fahrenheit. Uranus is made up of hydrogen, helium, ammonia, and methane. The methane makes Uranus blue. It is surrounded by several faint rings and has 27 moons. It takes Uranus 84 Earth years to complete 1 orbit around the sun. Uranus rotates in a clockwise direction, and is the only planet that spins on its side. A day on Uranus lasts 17 hours and 14 minutes.

8. Neptune is the furthest planet from the sun. It is made up of water, methane, and ammonia. Neptune is blue, because the methane absorbs red light and reflects blue light. Neptune is surrounded by faint rings and has 14 moons. It takes Neptune 165 Earth years to complete 1 orbit around the sun. It has the longest year of all planets. Neptune spins counterclockwise on its **axis**. A day in Neptune lasts 16 hours.

Did you know: The sun is a star, but it is not the biggest star in our solar system. Its **diameter** is about 865,370 miles compared to Earth's diameter of about 7,917.5 miles. The sun is about 93 million miles away from Earth. The Sun's core is the hottest part at about 27 million degrees Fahrenheit. It is the hottest place in the solar system. The sun is entirely gaseous and does not have any solid **surface**. The sun rotates on its axis in a counterclockwise direction about once every 26 days.

What's that sound? I hear someone calling.
That's my mommy. It was **stellar** to meet you, June.
Come back soon!
My name is Bella Bell, by the way. Time to go home and start a new day.

"spirals and swirls, dazzling flashes"

"sparkling colors, and floating shapes"

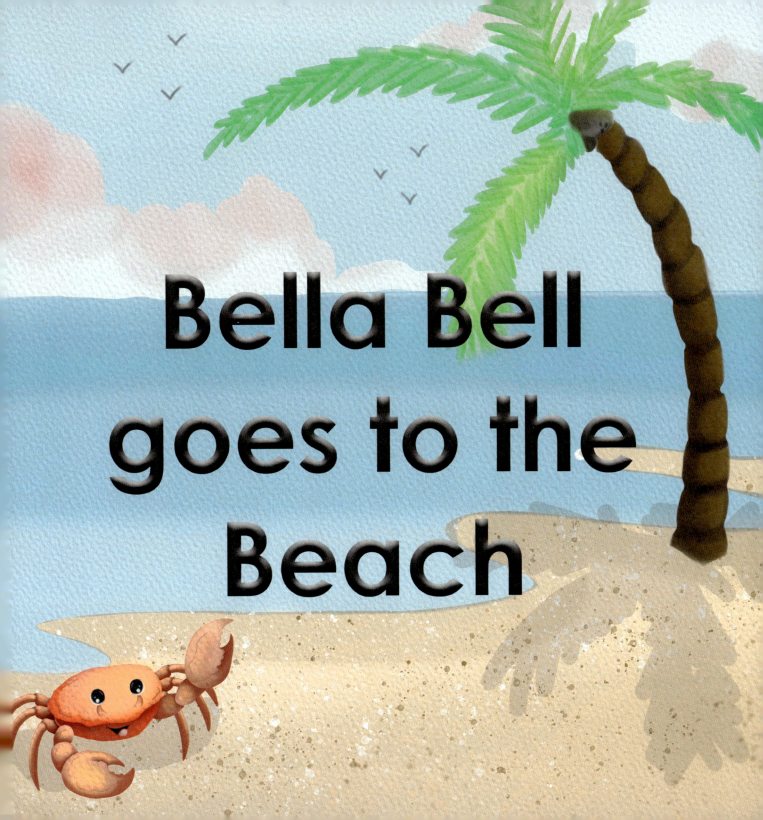

Bella Bell is at a breathtaking beach with her granny, Raquel. "I promised you a day of **delightful** fun under the **radiant** sun."

Thank you, granny. I won't go too far. I want to see. I want to explore. What lies beneath, what lies below. Into the big blue sea, I go.

Hello octopus, hello shark, hello whale.
I'm Bella Bell, please tell me a tale.

I am an **octagonal** octopus.
I have 8 legs, or is it 8 arms?
If ever I should lose one to a **foe**, it will surely regrow.
Sensitive suckers on my arms help me taste and smell.
What do you think, Bella Bell? Isn't that **swell**?
They act like small brains. Perhaps that explains
why each arm alone acts like it has a mind of its own.
I have blue blood and 3 hearts. These are the things that set me apart.

"How many tickles does it take to make an octopus laugh?"

"Ten-tickles"

Did you know: Octopuses have three hearts and blue blood. One heart circulates (moves continuously) blood around its body, and the other two hearts pump the blood past its **gills**. Octopuses have copper in their blood, making it blue, while humans have iron in their blood. They are boneless **creatures**, which help them fold and squeeze into tight spaces. In contrast, a human baby has about 300 bones at birth.

They eventually **fuse** together to 206 bones that make up an adult skeleton. 66% of the neurons (send and receive signals from the brain) are found in its arms. The arms of an octopus are full of suckers or suction cups that have **receptors**.

These receptors are very **sensitive** and can taste and touch. They can do multiple things at once with their arms. Octopuses are able to regrow lost arms. Male octopuses die a few months after mating. Female octopuses die shortly after giving birth. Octopuses can change the color of their body to **camouflage** with its surroundings. Some octopuses have an ink sac made up of melanin. Humans also have melanin, which is responsible for the color of our hair and skin.

Octopuses use their ink when feeling **threatened**. They **release** large amounts of ink into the water. This ink creates a dark cloud that can hurt the predator's eyes. Meanwhile, the octopus can get away from the predator.

Ready to **embark** on a **journey** with a **shifty** shark?
You can find me deep in the dark or above in the **shallow** ocean.
I **cruise** in slow **motion**.
My **gills** help me breathe. I have hundreds of teeth.
I **reproduce** a tooth for every one I lose.
Imagine my smile, you can see it from a mile.
My sharp **sense** of smell suits me well from afar.
Some call them **bizarre**, but I call them **divine**, the **critters** you'll find
on both sides of the **shoreline**.

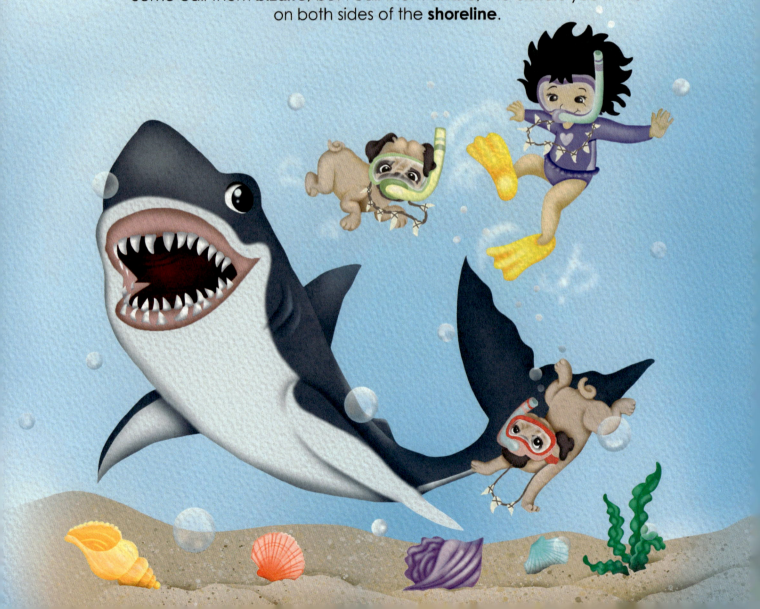

Did you know: There are about 500 **species** of sharks. They can be found in all five of Earth's oceans, at different depths, and **temperatures**. Some live in **shallow** water, while others live in water so deep that the sun never reaches them. Sharks come in different shapes and sizes. The largest shark is the whale shark. Whale sharks average a **length** of about 40 feet. In comparison, the average bus is about 40 feet long.

The dwarf lantern shark is the smallest shark, and it can fit in a human hand. Sharks do not have any bones in their bodies. They are made up of cartilaginous tissue. Human ears are also made up of cartilage. They are **nocturnal creatures** who can see really well at night. The back of their eyeballs have a reflective layer of tissue called a tapetum. This helps sharks see extremely well with little light.

Sharks go into tonic **immobility** when they are turned upside down, which means they enter a state of natural **paralysis**. Sharks can have up to 15 rows of teeth at once and up to 50,000 teeth in their lifetime. They have the ability to regrow teeth as they lose them. In comparison, humans have 32 teeth. Sharks do not have **lungs**, but they still need to breathe oxygen to survive.

They use their **gills** to remove oxygen from the water and get rid of **carbon dioxide**. Up to 66% of the total weight of a shark's brain is dedicated to smell. Some sharks can detect the blood of **prey** from a huge distance (one part of blood to one million parts of water). Sharks usually swim at a lower **speed** of about 1.5 miles per hour, but they swim much faster in short **pounces** when they are attacking at about 30 miles per hour.

Bella Bell, welcome to the splashy **splendid** sea.
Quite **spectacular**, don't you agree?
Come near, Come close.
I want you to hear about a **captivating creature**. I'll be your teacher.
This **wonderful** beast loves to **feast**. It gets a thrill off eating 40 million krill.
And the fun has just begun. It's got you beat by a **whopping** 200 tons.
Capable of breaking a scale. Can you imagine its trail?
Does my size give away my **disguise**? I am a blue whale, **wondrous** from head to tail.

Did you know: The **Baleen**, Antarctic blue whale, is the biggest animal on the planet, weighing up to 400,000 pounds and reaching about 100 feet in **length**. In comparison, the National Basketball Association (NBA) court is 94 feet long. There are two groups of whales: toothed and baleen. Toothed whales have teeth, which are used to hunt and eat squid, fish, and seals. Baleen whales have baleen instead of teeth which they use to collect shrimp-like krill, plankton, and small fish from the sea.

Baleen is made out of keratin, the same protein that makes up human fingernails and hair. These bristly baleen plates filter and trap **prey** from seawater inside their mouths. Baleen whales are usually larger than toothed whales. Whales cannot breathe underwater.

They use their blowholes to breathe air. A whale's heart weighs about 400 pounds. This is 640 times bigger than a human heart. Their tongues can weigh as much as an elephant. The blue whale has the largest **mammary glands** on Earth. Each is about 5 feet long and weighs as much as a baby elephant. Blue whale mothers can produce 440 pounds of milk per day. Blue whales can live to be about 90 years old.

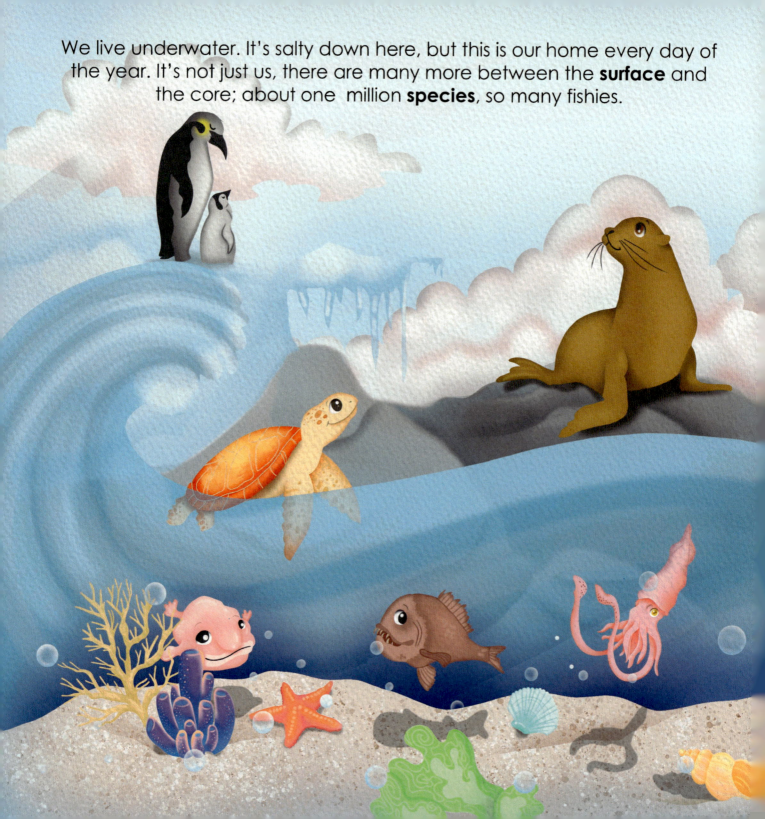

We live underwater. It's salty down here, but this is our home every day of the year. It's not just us, there are many more between the **surface** and the core; about one million **species**, so many fishies.

Did you know:

1. Anglerfish live in the deepest parts of the ocean, where the water is cold, the pressure reaches **colossal** values, and the amount of food is minimal. Its head occupies most of its body, and it has a huge mouth with sharp teeth. It can swallow **prey** that is twice as large as the body of the anglerfish itself. They can grow up to 3.3 feet long. This fish gets its name "angler" because of the growth that can be found only on the head of females. The rod is called the illicium, and at the end of it, there is an esca or bait. It is filled with mucus with **bioluminescent** (production of light by a living organism) bacteria, causing the bait to glow. It is used to lure prey. Male anglerfish **parasitize** on the females. Males have exceptional olfactory **senses** (relating to the sense of smell), which allow them to find females in darkness. The male attaches its teeth to the body of the female, and over time, males completely lose their **independence**. After parasitism, the only organ that continues to work in males is the genital organ, necessary for **breeding**. There can be several parasitic males attached to one female anglerfish at a time. All of them feed at the expense of the female, **fusing** with her circulatory systems.

2. Flying fish glide through the air. They swim fast underwater at a **speed** of about 37 miles per hour. The flying fish swims at an upward angle until it breaks through the **surface** water. It then begins to beat its tail swiftly, and its **pectoral** fins spread like wings. Flying fish can glide at a height of about 4 feet and reach a distance of about 600 feet. In comparison, the **length** of a football field is 360 feet. Flying fish break through the surface water and glide through the air to avoid **predators** chasing them underwater.

3. A Jellyfish isn't a fish at all. Fish are vertebrates and breathe through **gills**. Jellyfish are **invertebrates** and breathe by absorbing oxygen from the water through membranes. Jellyfish do not have brains, hearts, bones, or eyes. They can be clear, colorful, or bioluminescent. They have tentacles that sting and stun. This is helpful in defense of predators or in capturing **prey**. A Jellyfish is made up of 95% water. Proteins, muscles, and nerve cells make up the other 5%. In comparison, humans are made up of 60% water. A jellyfish out of water will **evaporate** and almost disappear. The box jellyfish has the most poisonous sting of all jellyfish. Its tentacles are covered with poisonous darts that can be deadly to humans. The lion's mane jellyfish is the world's largest jellyfish **species**. It can have tentacles that are up to 120 feet long. This is longer than the size of a blue whale which is the biggest mammal in the world.

4. Sea turtles cannot retract their heads and flippers into their shells. They cannot breathe underwater, but they can hold their breath for several hours. They often sleep underwater. Sea turtles spend the majority of their life at sea and will only return to land to nest. Sea turtles lay hundreds of eggs per nest. The nest's **temperature** determines the sex of the **hatchlings**. Cooler incubation temperatures produce male hatchlings, and warmer incubation temperatures produce female hatchlings. After the eggs hatch, the baby turtles will make their way towards the open ocean. Sea turtles can live to be about 50 years old.

5. The blobfish lives deep in the ocean at a depth of about 3,000 feet. It bobs along the ocean floor, scooping up small **creatures** that float across its path. The flesh of a blobfish is a gelatinous (jelly) mass. It does not have any bones or teeth. Blobfish grow to be up to 12 inches long. The female lays thousands of small pink eggs on the seafloor, and both males and females will sit on the eggs to protect them from predators. Blobfish cannot handle the decrease in pressure when brought to the surface or out of water. Their bodies begin to lose shape and appear as a blob.

6. Tasselled wobbegong sharks are also called carpet sharks because they resemble carpets. They are flat in shape and have lobes that look like whiskers hanging from their heads to their pectoral fins. Their shape and appearance are beneficial when hiding from predators or lying in wait for prey. The carpet shark lays on the ocean floor, **camouflaged** as if it were a carpet on the floor. When its prey comes close, the tasselled wobbegong attacks with a swift surprise attack. The tasselled wobbegong has 3 rows of sharp teeth in its upper jaw and two rows of teeth in its lower jaw. Carpet sharks can grow to be about 4 feet long.

7. Fangtooth fish are dark in color and have spiky scales all over their bodies. Their heads are big, and their bodies are small. The most noticeable feature of the fangtooth fish is its giant fangs. They have large, sharp, needle-like teeth that are the biggest out of any animal in the ocean when compared to the size of their body. The Fangtooth fish has two long fangs in its lower jaw. These two fangs are so long that opposing **sockets** have **evolved** on both sides of the brain so that the teeth can be **accommodated** when its jaw closes. Fangtooth fish live deep in the ocean at around 6,500 feet deep. They can grow to be about 6 inches long.

8. Just like Octopuses, squids also have 3 hearts, blue blood, 8 arms, and can **regenerate** lost arms. However, squids have 2 tentacles, which octopus do not have. A squid's tentacles are longer than its arms and are used to catch **prey**. They can grip and climb up **vertical surfaces** out of the water using their tentacles. Squids have sharp pointed beaks. They swim the fastest out of all invertebrates. The **colossal** squid and giant squid are the biggest of its **species** and can grow to be more than 40 feet in **length**. Squids have the biggest eyes out of any animal in the world when compared to their body size. Vampire Squids have 8 webbed arms that each have two rows of spines. The bottom of their arms are covered in suckers. The vampire squid can **propel** forward by **ejecting** water. This movement is called jet propulsion.

9. Penguins are flightless seabirds. They spend half their time in the ocean and the other half on land. A group of penguins in the water is called a raft, but on land, they are called a waddle. Penguins can hold their breath underwater for about 20 minutes and are excellent swimmers. This is because of how **streamlined** their body is. Their flippers act like propellers when underwater and allow the penguin to move forward and increase its **speed**. Their webbed feet get pushed away near the tail and are used to **navigate** through the water. The feathers are tightly packed and covered in oil, which keeps water out. Penguins are found on all continents in the southern hemisphere below the equator. The Galapagos Penguin is the only penguin **species** that will be found north of the equator in the **wild**. The Emperor Penguin is the tallest and can grow as tall as 4 feet. They can be found in the sea ice of Antarctica.

10. Seals, Sea Lions, and Walruses make up the pinniped group. Pinniped means fin or flipper. This group of mammals live in the ocean, but can be on land for long periods. They have a thick layer of fat called blubber. Blubber helps **marine** animals in cold **temperatures** by acting as **insulation**. Sea lions have ear flaps whereas seals do not have ear flaps. Walruses have tusks that can be as long as 3 feet. The tusks are used in defense and to cut through ice.

11. Sea Otters have the thickest fur of any animal. They can have up to 1 million hair follicles per square inch. In comparison, the average human head has about 100,000 hair follicles. Their thick fur keeps them warm, since they do not have any blubber. The sea otter is the only sea mammal to catch fish with its paws instead of its mouth. Sea Otters hold paws with each other and entangle themselves in seaweed to keep from floating away in the drifting sea. Although they can walk on land, sea otters spend almost all their time out in the open water.

12. Sea Stars are often called starfish, but they aren't actually fish. Sea Stars are shaped like stars, and most have 5 arms. However, some can have as many as 40 arms, like the Sun Star. Sea Stars can **regenerate** arms if they lose one. They do not have blood or brains and come in different shapes, sizes, and colors. The Sea Star can eat prey larger than itself by pushing its stomach through its mouth to the outside. It will then **digest** the food through its stomach, and when finished, it will push its stomach back down through its mouth. Sea Stars have one eye at the end of every arm that can see light and dark shades.

*An apex **predator** is a **species** that is at the top of the food chain and does not have any natural **predators** in its environment. The apex **predators** of the ocean are: killer whale, great white shark, leopard seal, sea lion, sperm whale, coconut crab, giant moray, whale shark, Atlantic torpedo ray.

Bella Bell and her magnifying glass

Bella Bell has counted sheep and fallen deep asleep...

It's 7 a.m. What a beautiful morning! The birds are chirping, the sun is shining, the dogs are whining, louder and louder.
Suddenly Bella Bell wakes up. She looks to her left, then looks to her right.
With a yawn, she looks towards her lawn.
It's my pugs sniffing bugs!

What do you smell? What do you see?
Is it a bee, or is it a flea?
What's in the grass?
Let's use my **magnifying** glass and insect book, so we can take a closer look.

All bugs are insects, but not all insects are bugs. Bugs are a type of insect and part of the order Hemiptera. All insects are found under the Insecta class. Insects have three body parts, six legs, four wings, and two antennae (a pair of long, thin sensory **appendages** on the head). While bugs have three life stages, most insects have four. Insects start off as eggs, then larvae (immature form), then pupa, and finally adults. In the pupa stage, they are sealed inside a cocoon and experience significant biological changes until adulthood. True bugs go through an incomplete **metamorphosis** which means they start off as eggs, hatch as nymphs (immature form), and then turn into an adult. Bugs do not go through the pupa stage.

Insect

- 3 body segments: a head, a thorax, and an abdomen
- 6 legs
- wings
- antennae
- life cycle: complete metamorphosis - egg → larva → pupa → adult

Arachnid

- 2 body parts: a cephalothorax and an abdomen
- 8 legs
- wingless
- no antennae
- life cycle: incomplete metamorphosis - egg → immature → adult

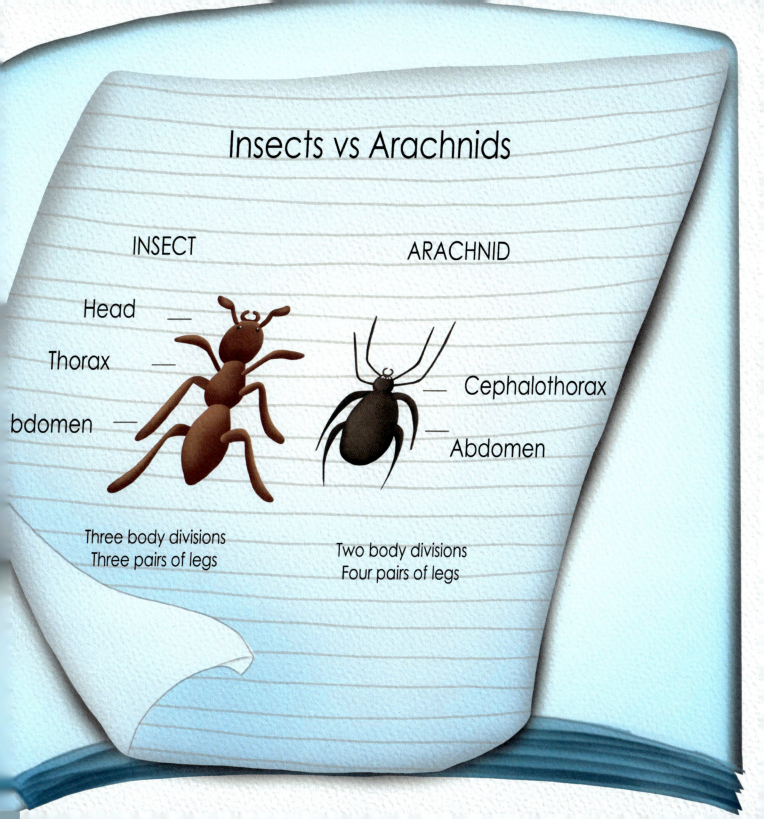

1. There are more than 3,000 **species** of walking stick bugs around the world. The walking stick is one of the biggest insects in the world. It can grow to be about 21 inches long. The walking stick bug has **evolved** to **camouflage** with its habitat and looks like a twig or branch. The walking stick bug can break off its leg at the joint and **regenerate** its **limb**. This is very helpful when escaping from **predators**. The female walking stick can **reproduce** without a male. This is called asexual reproduction.

2. Bees create colonies that include one fertile (able to produce) female queen bee, thousands of fertile male drone bees, and thousands of sterile (not able to produce) female worker bees. Bees work as a team to turn flower **nectar** into honey. Forager (to search or hunt) bees drink flower nectar so that the **enzymes** can break down the nectar sugar. The bee then regurgitates (to throw up or vomit) the nectar into a cell of the honeycomb. Bees fan the nectar by flapping their wings to **evaporate** any water and create sweet liquid honey. Bees can flap their wings about 200 beats per second.

3. Butterflies start off as caterpillars. A female butterfly lays hundreds of eggs in her lifetime. When an egg hatches, a caterpillar is born. The caterpillar spins a silky thread to build a cocoon around itself. Once inside the cocoon, the caterpillar **digests** itself. Some of the caterpillar's tissue survives the digestive process to create a new body. Once the butterfly is ready to break out of the cocoon, it **releases** fluid to soften the cocoon and pushes the cocoon walls until it breaks free and flies away.

4. Fireflies are **nocturnal** winged beetles with two pairs of wings. They are **bioluminescent**, which means they have the ability to light up. Firefly light can be yellow, green, or orange. Fireflies flash light patterns to attract mates and to scare off predators. The light is created by a chemical reaction. A firefly's light is a cold light. It generates very little heat. In comparison, a light bulb produces a lot of heat in addition to light. If a firefly's light-producing organ got as hot as a light bulb, the firefly would not survive the experience. One-hundred percent of the energy created is released through the light, making it the most **efficient** light in the world.

5. Rosy Maple Moths are pink, yellow, white, furry, and fluffy. They have antennas that look like feathers. Rosy maple moths are found in forests and live on maple trees. 24 hours after mating, females lay up to 200 eggs underneath a leaf. The eggs hatch larvae 2 weeks later. The larva will go through 5 stages of transformation before becoming a rosy maple moth. In the first 3 stages, the larvae live and eat together. In the 4th stage, they begin to eat **independently**. After another 10 to 14 days, they become pupae, which last 4 to 7 days. Lastly, adult rosy maple moths come out from pupae. The larvae and pupae feed on the maple tree, but adult rosy maple moths do not eat at all.

6. Ants live in colonies led by a queen ant. The queen ant lays millions of eggs in her lifetime. Worker ants are females that do not mate. Worker ants have many duties within the colony, like gathering food and caring for the queen's **offspring**. The male ants have one duty and that is to mate with the queen. Colonies can be as small as only a dozen ants or as big as millions of ants. When the queen ant dies, the colony dies soon after, because there is no one left to **reproduce**. Ants can live to be up to 30 years old and can carry up to 50 times their own weight. The Asian weaver ant is the strongest and can carry up to 100 times its own weight. There are more than 12,000 species of ants in the world.

7. Scorpions are not insects and are actually part of the arachnid family. They have two body parts and 4 pairs of legs. Scorpions give birth to live babies, unlike insects who lay eggs. Scorpions have one of the longest lifespans of all arthropods. On average, they can live about ten years in the **wild** and about 25 years in captivity. Scorpions can live without food for about a year and can hold their breath for about 6 days.

8. Tarantulas are the biggest spiders in the world. They come in a wide range of shapes, colors, and sizes. There are over 800 **species** of tarantulas. The biggest tarantula in the world is the goliath birdeater. It can grow up to 1 foot long. Male tarantulas have an average lifespan of 5 years, while female tarantulas can live up to 30 years. Tarantulas are **nocturnal** hunters but have poor eyesight. They sense through vibrations. The tarantula's size determines the size of its meal. It **preys** on insects, frogs, lizards, and snakes.

9. The funnel-web spider is one of the deadliest spiders in the world. It spins funnel-web shaped webs of silk that can be as deep as 25 inches. The funnel shaped web allows the spider to hide at the very bottom and wait for prey to fall in. Its prey includes cockroaches, beetles, millipedes, snails, frogs, and lizards. Once the prey has fallen victim, the funnel-web spider **pounces** and sinks its fangs in. Its fangs are sharp and strong. They can pierce a human fingernail. The male funnel-web spider's **venom** is 6 times more toxic than the female's venom. The venom is made up of neurotoxin atracotoxin. It attacks the nervous system and affects the organs.

10. The praying mantis is the only insect that can move its head and see 360 degrees. It can rotate its head 180 degrees on the left and right side. The praying mantis is a great jumper. It can twist and bend midair to land precisely on its intended target. It uses the spikes on its legs to pin down its prey. It can **camouflage** to look like a leaf, stick, flower, and different colors. Praying mantises are great hunters and eat their prey live. They feed on insects, spiders, frogs, lizards, and birds.

11. There are more than 11,000 species of grasshoppers in the world. Grasshoppers are usually green or brown, so they can camouflage with grass or dirt. Their ears are located on their **abdomen**. Grasshoppers can jump as far as 30 inches. In comparison, if humans were able to jump as far as grasshoppers, then we would jump more than the **length** of a football field in a single bound. A grasshopper's **hind** legs act like springs. The grasshopper will relax its bended knee to fling into the air. Grasshoppers are great jumpers, but can also use their wings to fly.

12. Did You Know: Snails and slugs are not insects; they are mollusks. They are **invertebrates**, which means they do not have a skeleton. Snails have a protective shell on their backs which slugs do not have. Snails and slugs do not have legs. They let out a mucus substance that allows them to slide from one place to another. Snails and slugs are hermaphrodites, which means they have both male and female reproductive organs. The giant whelk snail is the biggest in the world, and it can grow to be over 2 feet long. The limax maximus is the biggest slug in the world, and it can grow as long as 3 feet. Snails and slugs travel very slowly. The whelk snail can move at **speeds** of about 4 inches per minute. The limax maximus slug can move at speeds of about 6 inches per minute.

The world is BIG, and LIFE is GRAND.

Friends are found high in the sky and down underground.

Some of us are tall, some of us are tiny.

Some of us are shy, and some of us are **mighty**.

But rest assured, we all share a place of birth on planet Earth, and the **splendor** that is the circle of life is bound to make the world go round, and that my friends is a **ginormous** fact, to be exact!

KINGDOM

Vertebrates (animals with a backbone)

1. **Amphibians**: frogs, toads, salamanders, newts
   - live on land and water
   - smooth, slimy, and moist skin
   - breathe through their skin and in some cases, their lungs
   - ectothermic (cold-blooded) regulation of body temperature depends on environment
   - most follow the life cycle of egg → larva → adult
   - fertilize eggs externally, some internally.
2. **Birds**: eagles, owls, parrots, penguins, ostriches
   - all birds have wings, but not all birds can fly
   - bipedal (have 2 legs)
   - bodies are covered in feathers
   - endothermic (warm-blooded) maintain constant body temperature
   - lay eggs
   - beak with no teeth
3. **Fish**: sharks, flying fish, seahorse, clownfish
   - all fish live in water
   - all fish have gills (gills absorb oxygen from water and release carbon dioxide to breathe)
   - ectothermic (cold-blooded) regulation of body temperature depends on environment
   - the swim bladder organ helps ensure fish don't sink or float
   - fins provide motion, maneuverability, and stability
4. **Mammals**: dogs, monkeys, whales, bats
   - covered in hair or fur
   - endothermic (warm-blooded) maintain constant body temperature
   - mammals nurse their young with milk produced by mammary glands
   - lower jawbone (dentary) is a single piece, hinged directly to the skull
   - give birth to live young (except the platypus and the echidna)
5. **Reptiles**: lizards, crocodiles, turtles, snakes
   - live on land and water
   - bodies covered with scales
   - ectothermic (cold-blooded) regulation of body temperature depends on environment
   - produce shelled eggs or give birth to live young.
   - 4 legs or descended from animals with 4 legs.
   - breathe through lungs

ANIMALIA

Invertebrates (animals without a backbone)
Over 95% of all animals on Earth are invertebrates.

1. **Arthropods**: crabs, scorpions, insects, spiders, centipedes
   - jointed limbs and an exoskeleton
   - the largest phylum in the animal kingdom
   - exoskeletons made of chitin

2. **Cnidarians**: jellyfish, corals, anemones, hydra
   - stinging cells
   - live in water
   - radially symmetrical

3. **Echinoderms**: sea stars, brittle stars, sea urchins, sea cucumbers
   - spiny skin
   - live in water
   - skeleton is made up of calcium carbonate
   - five sided radial symmetry

4. **Mollusks**: snails, clams, squids, octopus
   - soft bodies
   - unsegmented bodies
   - hard exoskeleton

5. **Poriferans**: sponges
   - multicellular organisms
   - live in water
   - lack complex organs

6. **Annelids**: earthworms, leeches, lugworms
   - segmented and muscular body
   - hydrostatic skeleton
   - primitive brain
   - digestive systems stretch from the mouth to the anus

GLOSSARY - a short dictionary relating to a specific subject or text

12 inches = 1 foot → 3 feet = 1 yard → 1,760 yards = 1 mile
212 degrees Fahrenheit = **boiling point**
32 degrees Fahrenheit = **freezing point**
abdomen - the belly
abound - exist in large numbers or amounts
accommodate - to provide enough space
amazing - causing great surprise or wonder
amphibian - able to live both on land and in water
appendage - a thing that is added or attached to something larger
astonishing - extremely surprising or impressive
axis - imaginary line about which a body rotates
baleen - whalebone made of keratin
bind - a problematical situation
bioluminescent - production of light by a living organism
bizarre - very strange or unusual
breed - animals or plants within a species
camouflage - to hide or disguise by covering up or changing the way it looks
capable - having the ability to do something
captivating - capable of attracting and holding interest
carbon dioxide - a colorless, odorless gas found in our atmosphere
clever - skilled at doing something
cognition - understanding through thought, experience, and the senses
colossal - extremely large
counterclockwise - the opposite direction the hands of a clock move around
creature - an animal
critters - a living animal
cruise - travel smoothly
decibel - a unit used to measure the intensity of a sound
delightful - great pleasure
diameter - a straight line passing from side to side through the center of a circle
digest - to break down substances that can be absorbed by the body
disguise - give a different appearance to hide one's identity
divine - excellent; delightful.
dominant - power over others
efficient - achieving maximum productivity with minimum wasted effort
eject - throw something in a sudden way
embark - to begin or start

enthralling - capturing and holding one's attention
enzyme - a substance that causes a biochemical reaction
evaporate - turn from liquid to vapor
evolve - develop from a simple to a more complex form
expand - become or make larger
extraordinary - very unusual or remarkable
exuberant - filled with lively energy and excitement
fahrenheit - a scale of temperature
fantastic - extraordinarily good
fascinating - extremely interesting
feast - a large meal
fiery - burning strongly and brightly
foe - enemy or opponent
function - an activity or purpose
fuse - join or blend to form a single entity
gem - a precious stone
gestation - the process of carrying or being carried in the womb
gills - a respiratory organ
ginormous - extremely large
glorious - worthy of admiration
guide - to show or indicate the way to someone
hatchling - a young animal that has recently emerged from its egg
herbivore - feeds on plants
hind - situated at the back
hollow - empty space inside
immobility - not being able to move
impressive - admiration through size, quality, or skill
incredible - impossible to believe
independent - self supporting, surviving without outside assistance
insulated - prevents the loss of heat
invertebrates - animals without a backbone
journey - traveling from one place to another
knockout - to defeat or stun
lactation - making milk
length - measurement of something from end to end
limb - an arm or leg
lungs - pair of organs within the rib cage
magical - supernatural
magnificent - impressively beautiful or extravagant

magnifying glass - a lens that produces an enlarged image
mammary gland - milk producing organ found in females
marine - found in the sea
marvelous - causing great wonder; extraordinary
mesmerizing - capturing one's complete attention
metamorphosis - the process of transformation from an immature form to an adult form
mighty - great power or strength, especially despite size
motion - the action of moving
nasal - relating to the nose
navigate - to plan and direct a route
nectar - a sugary fluid made by plants
nocturnal - active at night
octagonal - eight sided
offspring - a person's or animal's children
paralysis - not able to move
parasite - an organism that lives in or on an organism of another species
pectoral - relating to the breast or chest
pounce - spring or swoop suddenly to catch prey
powerful - having great power or strength
precious - of great value
predator - animal that naturally hunts other animals
prey - an animal that is hunted by another animal
propel - to push and move in a particular direction
radiant - sending out light; shining or glowing brightly
receptor - cells able to respond to stimulus and transmit a signal to a sensory nerve
regenerate - to replace lost or injured tissue
release - to let go
remarkable - worthy of attention
reproduce - create something very similar to something else
retain - to keep
roam - move or travel
salutations - a greeting or acknowledgment of another's arrival or departure
scavenging - search for and collect
science - a systematically organized body of knowledge on a particular subject
sense - sight, smell, hearing taste, touch
sensitive - quick to detect or respond to slight changes
shallow - not very deep
shifty - dodging movements
shoreline - the line along which a large body of water meets the land

slither - to move smoothly over a surface
snout - the nose and mouth of an animal
soaring - flying or rising high in the air
socket - a hollow into which something fits
solitary - alone
special - better, greater, or otherwise different from what is usual
species - a group of living organisms consisting of similar individuals
spectacular - beautiful in a dramatic and eye-catching way
speed - the rate at which someone or something is able to move or operate
sphere - a round solid figure with every point on its surface equidistant from its center
splendid - magnificent; very impressive
splendor - magnificent features or qualities
starry - full of or lit by stars
stellar - relating to the stars, brilliant, outstanding
strange - unusual, surprising, or hard to understand
streamlined - having a form that has very little resistance to a flow of air or water
strength - being physically strong
suckle - to feed a baby or young animal
suffocate - cause to die from lack of air
surface - the outside part or uppermost layer of something
swell - excellent; very good
temperature - the degree of heat present in a substance or object
threatened - express one's intention to harm
thrive - grow or develop well
translucent - allowing light, but not detailed shapes, to pass through; semitransparent
unique - being the only one of its kind
vegetation - plants in a particular area or habitat
venomous - a poisonous substance
vertebrates - animals with a backbone
vertical - the direction where the top is directly above the bottom
vision - the state of being able to see
whim - a sudden desire or change of mind
whopping - very large
wild - living or growing in the natural environment; not domesticated
wonderful - inspiring delight, pleasure, or admiration
wondrous - inspiring a feeling of wonder or delight
zany - amusingly bizarre

It's been my lifelong dream to write a children's book. It wasn't until my niece, Bella, was born that I felt motivated to actually start. I felt a fire lit under me and I was inspired to write this book for all of you. Each and every person and situation I have encountered has molded my perspective. I am really thankful for the people and experiences I have lived through during the two years it took to realize this dream. May the future always look hopeful and may we rejoice in our existence.

Susana Aguilar

Made in the USA
Middletown, DE
23 February 2023